THE LAND SOUTHWARD

For Marvin

THE LAND SOUTHWARD
A Play in Two Acts

By Darcy Hogan

© 2005 by Darcy Hogan

ISBN 978-1-257-06878-4

Please see page vi for further copyright information.

THE LAND SOUTHWARD

First performed at The Hunger Artists Theatre Company,
Fullerton, CA, April 1st – 24th, 2005,
produced by The March Hog Theater Company,
with the following cast members:

Joe	Jason Lythgoe
Maggie	Erin Michaeli
The Man	Michael Serna
Liz	Abbie De Vera Jackson
May	Joyce Ericksen
The Boy	Jeremy Gable
The Girl	Kimberly K. Mitchell

Directed by Darcy Hogan

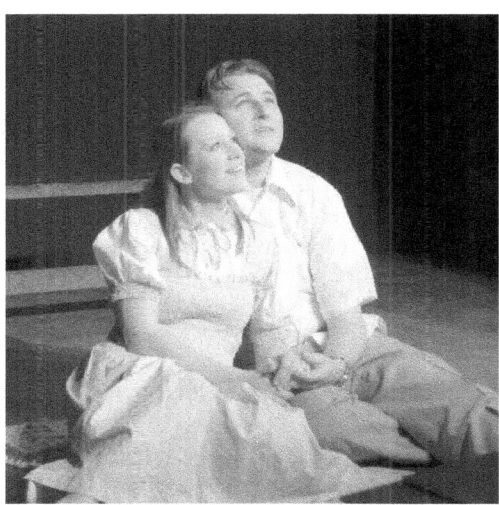

Erin Michaeli & Jason Lythgoe

COPYRIGHT INFORMATION

(See also page iv)

This play is fully protected under the Copyright Laws of the United States of America and all countries of the Berne and Universal Copyright Conventions. All rights including Stage, Motion Picture, Radio, Television, Public Reading, and Translation into Foreign Languages, as strictly reserved.

Licenses for all performances are issued subject to the understanding that the name of the author of the play shall be included on ALL advertising, programs, electronic or printed materials and shall appear no less than 40% the size of the title of the play, in a font no smaller than 12pt; and that the integrity of the authors' work will be preserved.

In no way, at any time, is it acceptable to alter this script in any way. This play must be performed as written, as intended herein by the author, and no changes (in text or intent) may be made without specific, written permission from the author herself.

The Royalty Fee for this play is subject to contract and variation at the discretion of the author. Lesser fees may apply to bona fide Non-Profit organizations. In Theaters or Halls seating four-hundred or more persons, the fee will be subject to negotiation.

VIDEO RECORDING OF PRODUCTIONS

Please note that the copyright laws governing video-recording are extremely complex and it should not be assumed that any play may be video-recorded, for whatever purpose, without first obtaining the permission of the appropriate agents. The fact that a play is published does not indicate that video rights are available, nor that the publisher controls such rights.

CHARACTERS:

JOE: 20s to 30s. Exists in 1950s. Joe is a young, energetic Mormon man from Southern Utah. He joins the Army and is assigned to Camp Desert Rock Nevada). This actor will also play Joe's son in one scene.

MAGGIE: 20s to 30s. Exists in 1950s. Joe's wife. A young Mormon woman, also from Southern Utah. Naive, caring, honest and faithful.

MAY: 60s. Exists in early 1990s. She is a strong woman. A downwind survivor and widow who is dying. She gives her story to Liz.

LIZ: 20s to 30s. Exists in early 1990s. A young, rebellious writer from Los Angeles who comes to Utah determined to blow the lid off the "downwind conspiracy."

THE MAN: Any Age. Exists in all time periods. He really is "The Man." An Army Lieutenant, a police officer, a Mormon bishop, an Atomic Energy Commission head, a politician, a doctor, a game show host, etc. Role requires a very strong actor with good comic timing -- one capable of a menacing presence.

THE GIRL: 20s to 40s. Exists in all time periods. Plays many roles. A friend, housewife, reporter, game show contestant, waitress, student, etc. Requires a very versatile actor.

THE BOY: 20s to 40s. Exists in all time periods. Plays many roles. A husband, businessman, news reporter, game show contestant, scientist, etc. Requires a very versatile actor.

NOTE: Transitions between time periods can be accomplished with differences in lighting, costumes, music, etc.

With special thanks to Kate Boyes, Dr. Xan Johnson,
Kay Cook, Eric Eberwein, Johnna Adams,
David Mong, Kelly Flynn and Russ Marchand.

- 0 -

ACT I

> *Lights up. There is a bench USC, a rocking chair SL, a desk SR. LIZ stands SR, looking at old documents. MAY is SL, sweeping. Dust wafts into the air toward LIZ.*

MAY: I'm not going to tell you my story. I'm going to tell you yours. Ours.

LIZ: 1950 to 1963.

MAY: A housewife speaks in Utah. Do you hear?

LIZ: Why didn't anyone say anything? Do anything?

MAY: We were taught to believe.

LIZ: It's so odd.

MAY: So odd how a lie becomes truth.

LIZ: The story's out there. It's still there.

MAY: But stories find their way. As if the Universe had a hand. As if they were written on the wind.

LIZ: Are you ready?

MAY: It's time.

> *Lights fade. We hear exciting music. As LIZ and MAY exit, images of Southern Utah are projected across the stage.*

THE MAN (V.O.): Welcome to beautiful Southern Utah. Gateway to the National Parks. A sprawling desert oasis in the heart of the Southwest. From her red rock canyons to her snowy mountain peaks, this is Southern Utah!

Throughout this, THE MAN enters
and stands C, facing US. JOE,
MAGGIE, THE GIRL and THE BOY
enter and stand US facing DS. They
hold hymnals. Music and images fade,
lights rise.

ALL:
(*Singing.*)

We'll find the place that God for us prepared,
Far away, in the west.
Where none shall come to hurt or make afraid;
There the saints will be blessed.
We'll make the air with music ring,
Shout praises to our God and King;
Above the rest these words we'll tell,
All is well! All is well!

THE MAN: (*To the others.*) First Nephi, Chapter 2, verse twenty. "And inasmuch as ye shall keep my commandments, ye shall prosper, and shall be led to a land of promise; yea, even a land which I have prepared for you; yea, a land which is choice above all other lands."

ALL: Amen.

Blackout. THEY exit. Spotlight on
MAY who sits in a rocking chair.

MAY: It was all in the timing. Oh, they picked the right crowd. We weren't pushy. We didn't cause trouble. In fact, if there was a way to put a curtain up around us, we'd have done it.(*Laughs.*) "The Zion Curtain." The Mormon life. People pretty much just wanted to keep to themselves. Keep on pretending the outside world didn't exist. Sure enough, we did pretty good keeping our heads in the sand.

Spot on MAY fades. SHE exits. Lights
up on JOE.

JOE: I was born in St. George in 1929. The second of five children. Named for our prophet, Joseph Smith. My parents moved to Southern Utah to start a family, and they couldn't have made a better choice. It was beautiful. From my front door you could see for miles. The grass in our front yard extended out exactly twenty-three steps from the porch stoop, and beyond that was nothing but warm, red desert. From my backyard you could see the St. George temple rising in the distance like a white castle, and I could sprint to my uncle's house and back in sixty-two seconds. I timed it. The skies were always clear and blue, even in the wintertime, and it never got too cold. It was perfect. Paradise. I didn't ever want to leave.

Lights fade on JOE. Lights up on MAGGIE and THE GIRL.

MAGGIE: (*To THE* GIRL.) I know Joe is in love with me. I know he wants to marry me, but he isn't going to ask until he figures out a way to make a living. His father makes a good living on the ranch, but that isn't for Joe.

THE GIRL: Why not?

MAGGIE: Joe doesn't like the slaughter house. Never did have the stomach for it.

Lights on MAGGIE and THE GIRL fade. THEY exit. Lights back up on JOE.

JOE: Maggie waited two years for me while I was on my mission. She wrote to me nearly every day. It wasn't fair for me to make her wait anymore. It was time for us to go to the Temple. Time for us to get married. But I had to find a job first, and there was no way I was going to spend my life like my father had. I couldn't live that way -- coming home every night with all that blood on my hands. So ... I decided to join up.

Lights up on THE MAN who stands US in a military uniform.

JOE: The Marines!

JOE turns and salutes THE MAN who then shakes his hand. We hear "Marine Corps Hymn," preferably sung by the Mormon Tabernacle Choir*.

** Cautionary Note: Rights to produce
this play do not include permission to
use these artists in production.*

*THE GIRL and THE BOY enter and
begin dressing JOE in a uniform.
THEY pantomime shaving his head.
THEY finish quickly and hand JOE a
rifle. THE BOY, THE GIRL and THE
MAN march in unison, stop, and
salute forward. Blackout. We hear
music playing, signifying a time shift
to the early 90s. Lights up on LIZ who
holds a phone. Waiting.*

LIZ: ... No, I'm still holding ..... thank you.(*Suddenly, she straightens
up.*)Yes, thank you. Did you get my fax? ..... but that's a steal, really, for
what you're getting ..... well, it started out as just an article, but there's too
much to ..... look, this is going to be big. Huge. I guarantee it ..... well, sure
but if you consider . ..... yes, I spoke with a woman in Cedar City who .....
well, I'll get more, but I need to be there. I have to find them. I have to look
around. That's where you come in. If I could just get a small cash advance,
I ..... well, what about half of it? ..... a quarter of it? ..... look, if I don't get
something I won't be able to ..... fine ..... no, I understand ..... I will ..... you
too.

*SHE hangs up the phone. SHE looks
around, frustrated, thinking. SHE
picks up a small voice recorder,
presses play, listens.*

MAY (V.O.): (*As if coming from voice recorder.*) My family moved here
from Pennsylvania in nineteen thirty-four. Nearly sixty years ago, now.

*Lights up on MAY in rocking chair.
Lights dim on LIZ.*

MAY: We weren't completely ignorant. I saw what was going on and --
well, you would really have to try not to see it. But most times I just bit my
tongue. Just the way I was raised, I guess. (*Beat.*) It's like when your

teenage daughter starts parking. You know, parking? With a boy? Well, you know she's doing it, and she knows she's doing it. But together you just pretend that it's not going on -- and that makes it okay. It's like an unspoken pact. You even hope and pray that she doesn't come out and tell you about it, because then you'll have to deal with it. And you don't want to deal with it. (*Beat.*) When they started testing the water over at Red Hill -- I thought that was more than a little odd. But the sheep ... just hundreds of them laying there in the fields, dying. Someone had to say something. (*Beat.*) We tried. Some did. They gave us excuses. Not even good ones. I didn't expect anything more than that, really. I just wanted to speak up. I just wanted them to know that someone was paying attention. (*Beat.*) But it's useless to get angry. After all, dyin's just a part of life.

> *Lights back up on LIZ, still holding the miniature tape recorder, listening.*

LIZ (V.O.): (*As if coming from voice recorder*) What was that?

MAY (V.O.): I say dying's just a part of life.

> *Beat.*

MAY: (*To Audience.*) Not the worst part, neither. Just the last part.

> *LIZ stops the tape. Lights dim on MAY. LIZ picks up the phone again, dials.*

LIZ: (*Waits, then --*) Hey, it's Liz ..... are you still interested in buying my car? .....

> *Lights out on LIZ. SHE and MAY exit. THE MAN enters in military uniform. HE puts on his hat. As he does, the lights come up. We are at Camp Desert Rock, a military base in Nevada. Two signs are displayed on the stage. One reading "If you wouldn't tell STALIN, don't tell ANYONE" and another reading*

> *"*Loose lips sink ships*". JOE rushes*
> *onto the stage and stands at attention.*

THE MAN: Thank you, gentlemen. It is my job to inform you of your duties here at Camp Desert Rock. I know many of you have questions. I will try to answer them for you. *(HE clears his throat, pulls a slip of paper from his breast pocket, and reads.)* "Gentleman, welcome to Nevada and Camp Desert Rock. We have selected each of you very carefully for this very important mission. You are the best of the best. You should consider yourself honored to be a part of this historic undertaking. Understand that the effort you put forth during your time here will undoubtedly echo across the globe. Keep your film-badge with you at all times . . . this will insure that your radiation levels remain normal. May we remind you that for each of you here today, there are at least a hundred soldiers who would gladly take your place. If you have any questions, you will refer to your manuals." *(HE slips the paper back into his pocket.)* Any questions?

> *JOE raises his hand.*

THE MAN: Dismissed.

> *THE MAN blows a whistle and exits.*
> *JOE lowers his hand as he watches*
> *THE MAN exit, then exits the opposite*
> *direction. Lights fade. Lights up.*
> *Sounds of an airport terminal. LIZ*
> *enters, carrying a suitcase. She sets it*
> *down and looks around.*

LIZ: It's pretty here. A little ... empty. But very pretty.

> *THE GIRL enters and begins to pass*
> *by LIZ. LIZ stops her.*

LIZ: Excuse me? How far is Cedar City from here?

THE GIRL: Oh, that's about four or five hours south of here.

LIZ: Is there a bus station nearby?

THE GIRL: It's all the way downtown.

LIZ: Walking distance?

THE GIRL: Oh, goodness no. I can drive you there.

LIZ: Oh, no. That's alright. I'll catch a cab.

THE GIRL: (*Grabs LIZ's bag and begins to walk off.*) Don't be silly, I'll give you a lift. I'm going that way anyhow.

LIZ: (*Without a choice, follows after her.*) Well ... okay. Thank you.

> *THEY exit. THE BOY enters and sits on the bench. LIZ re-enters now carrying a Book of Mormon and a Tupperware container. SHE sits beside THE BOY.*

THE BOY: Hello!

LIZ: Hello.

THE BOY: Where you headed?

LIZ: South.

THE BOY: No duh. Where?

LIZ: Cedar City.

THE BOY: Me, too! (*Points to her Tupperware container.*) Watcha' got there?

LIZ: Uh, something green. I don't really know.

THE BOY: You gonna' eat that?

LIZ: Not on your life.

> *SHE hands it to THE BOY who opens it and starts to eat -- green Jello with carrot slices.*

THE BOY: Thanks. So, I guess its lucky you sat next to me.

LIZ: Really? Why is that?

THE BOY: Well, I'm an R.M. Folks that ride these busses ... well, it's probably good you're not on your own anymore.

LIZ: What's an R.M.?

THE BOY: A returned missionary. So ... you're not LDS?

LIZ: L.D.S.?

THE BOY: I guess not then. LDS ... Latter-Day Saint. I saw your Book of Mormon there, so I thought --

LIZ: Oh! No, someone just gave this to me. It's not mine.

THE BOY: It is now.

LIZ: I guess you're right.

THE BOY: So ... what are you doing in Utah?

LIZ: Actually, I don't really know. I just quit school.

THE BOY: Gosh, that's too bad.

LIZ: Not really. To be honest, it wasn't my fault. My Lit professor's a real asshole.

> *THE BOY's eyes widen in surprise and HE looks around quickly to make sure no one else heard "that word." LIZ doesn't notice.*

THE BOY: So ... how long have you been in Salt Lake?

LIZ: About three hours.

THE BOY: Did you get to see Temple Square?

LIZ: Well, you can't really miss it, can you?

>*THE BOY looks away.*

LIZ: I'm sorry. That was a joke.

THE BOY: No, I get it. I get it.

LIZ: I'm a writer. I'm here to research a story.

THE BOY: Oh! You write for the newspapers?

LIZ: Uh, no. Just for me. For now at least.

THE BOY: Hmmm. Well, Heavenly Father gives us obstacles. We just have to roll with the punches and do our best. It's all in His hands.

LIZ: That easy, huh?

THE BOY: Sure! Take me for example.

LIZ: What do you mean?

THE BOY: Well, He gave me an arm that don't work.

>*LIZ notices he's not using one arm.*

LIZ: I'm sorry.

THE BOY: Nah. Don't be. It's okay. I do fine. It's just my personal trial. He's just testing me.

LIZ: For what?

THE BOY: Who knows? Or it could be a punishment.

LIZ: What the -- ... for what?

THE BOY: Who knows? Something I did maybe. He does that sometimes.

LIZ: You really think that HE would do that to you?

THE BOY: You never know. Everything happens for a reason. One time my sister's friend had an ...(*HE looks around, then whispers.*)Abortion. And the next day we had an earthquake.

LIZ: And you think those two things are related?

THE BOY: You never know. (*Beat.*)Hey, thanks for the Jello.

LIZ: No problem.

> *Lights out. Lights up on MAGGIE, who wears a wedding gown. SHE checks herself in an invisible mirror. THE GIRL rushes in with a sewing kit.*

THE GIRL: I've got it! Don't worry.

MAGGIE: I can't believe it! At least it's the right length.

THE GIRL: (*Kneeling down to pin the waist of Maggie's dress.*) It could be worse.

MAGGIE: Make it tighter.

THE GIRL: You don't want it too tight, you could faint.

MAGGIE: I'm not going to faint.

THE GIRL: You might faint.

MAGGIE: I won't faint! I've been practicing holding in my tummy all week. I want to look thin. Thin and beautiful.

THE GIRL: You are thin. AND beautiful. You look lovely, really.

MAGGIE: Hair up, or hair down?

THE GIRL: Um ... down. Up!

MAGGIE: Well, which is it?

THE GIRL: Up. Maybe we'll put some baby's breath in there. Wouldn't that be pretty?

> *MAGGIE toys with her hair in an imaginary mirror. THE GIRL finishes pinning and stands back.*

MAGGIE: I'm so excited!

THE GIRL: You should be!

MAGGIE: I want to look perfect for Joe. When I meet him at the Temple on Saturday --

THE GIRL: When does he get in?

MAGGIE: Not 'til Saturday morning.

THE GIRL: You're kidding. Not 'til then?

MAGGIE: Couldn't be helped. He's VERY important over there. It was all he could do to get the weekend off so we could have a honeymoon.

THE GIRL: When does he go back?

MAGGIE: Monday morning.

THE GIRL: (*Disappointed for her.*) Well, at least you have the weekend, right?

MAGGIE: Right. I'm still just so grateful he got stationed near by. Of all places, Nevada. It's just a few hours away. We are so blessed. I mean, imagine if we had to move away.

THE GIRL: I know.

MAGGIE: We're buying a house you know. Just like that! Joe is making so much money now. So much more than anyone else around here.

THE GIRL: So ... lots of babies?

MAGGIE: (*Laughing.*) Definitely. A whole house-full! But, not as many as my folks had. I don't know if we could handle that. We only want four or five.

> *MAGGIE sucks in her belly and poses in the imaginary mirror.*

THE GIRL: Whatever you do, DON'T lock your knees

> *Lights fade. They exit. THE MAN enters again as the Mormon Bishop, Book of Mormon in hand and glasses on. HE addresses the audience as his congregation.*

THE MAN: I would like to take a moment and welcome our newlyweds, Joseph and Margaret Anderson. They went before our Heavenly Father yesterday and were joined together for time and all eternity. Sealed in the Temple. All men holding the Aaronic Priesthood are invited to join us after the service today. We'll be laying our hands on the couple to bless their union and pray for children. Now, Brother Bentley would like me to remind you that there will be a meeting this Tuesday night at the town hall about the all the activity next door. I would encourage you all to attend. Free literature will be available, as well as punch and donuts. This is also your chance to get information on dates, times, and the best viewing locations.

> *Lights out. Lights up on LIZ. SHE sits on the bench. MAY enters, bringing her a glass of lemonade.*

MAY: I remember that meeting. I was married at the time. My husband, Peter and I were busy with the farm. We were blessed with work. (*SHE sits beside LIZ.*) But we took time out for this meeting. Got dressed up. Peter wanted to pick up a schedule so we'd know when to go watch. But we took time out for this meeting. Got dressed up. Peter wanted to pick up a schedule so we'd know when to go watch. We didn't get much information at the meeting, other than dates and times. That was about it. And they handed out pamphlets. Little fliers that were ... well, ridiculous really. Colorful, and they read like children's books. And that filmstrip ...(*SHE laughs.*)... something about a turtle and a Cub Scout? Oh, I don't remember anymore.

> *Lights out on MAY and LIZ. THEY exit. Strobe lights up. The words "ADAM THE ATOM: HE'S OUR FRIEND" are displayed somehow (projected, or on a card). We should get the impression we are watching a 1950s propaganda film. Sappy background music, filmstrip sounds. THE MAN enters wearing a 1950s suit jacket - fairly cheesy. HE holds a microphone.*

THE MAN: What is atomic energy? (*Pause.*) Hello friends, I'm Dick Newcomb. To help you better understand atomic energy, I've asked a friend of mine to join us today!

> *THE MAN pulls a hand puppet from his pocket and begins moving its "lips" as if to make it speak.*

THE MAN (AS PUPPET): Hello, Dick! I'm Adam the Atom!

THE MAN: Hello, Adam!

THE MAN (AS PUPPET): Hello, Dick!

THE MAN: Tell us, Adam, what is Atomic Energy?

THE MAN (AS PUPPET): Atomic Energy is the most wonderful resource in the world!

THE MAN: Really, and why is that, Adam?

- 14 -

THE MAN (AS PUPPET): Atomic energy is clean, safe, and can provide us with everything we'll ever need!

> *THE GIRL enters in 1950s era typical "housewife" outfit. She wears oven mitts and carries a pot roast.*

THE GIRL: Like electricity to run my stove?

THE MAN (AS PUPPET): Yep!

> *THE BOY enters wearing a 1950s era leisure suit. He carries a golf club and has a pipe in his mouth.*

THE BOY: And gas to run my shiny new automobile?

THE MAN (AS PUPPET): That's right!

THE GIRL: And curlers for my stylish hairdo?

THE MAN (AS PUPPET): You betcha'!

THE BOY: (*Swings the golf club.*) And tips to improve my swing?

THE MAN (AS PUPPET): Yessiree!

THE GIRL: What about lollipops for the kids?

THE MAN (AS PUPPET): You got it!

THE BOY: And beer for me and the boys?

THE MAN: Of course!

THE GIRL: And milk?

THE BOY: And cookies?

THE GIRL: And music?

THE BOY: And baseball?

THE GIRL: And love?

THE BOY: And harmony?

THE GIRL: And world peace?

THE MAN (AS PUPPET: You betcha'!

THE MAN: That's right, Adam, Atomic Energy gives us all that and more!

THE BOY: And, is Atomic Energy safe for ... my dog, Spot?

SPOT (V.O.): Woof!

THE MAN (AS PUPPET): Dogs love Atomic Energy!

THE BOY & THE GIRL: (*Together.*) And so do we!

THE MAN: Well, Adam! Sounds like Atomic Energy might just be the world's most perfect resource.

THE MAN (AS PUPPET): That's right, Dick. Perfect. Just like *you.*

THE MAN: (*Laughs, mock modesty.*) Aw, thanks Adam. And thank you, folks, for joining us tonight. And remember ...

ALL: The Atom is our friend!

> *ALL give the "thumbs up." Blackout.*
> *THEY exit. Lights up. LIZ is signing a*
> *piece of paper. THE BOY stands in*
> *front of her, waiting.*

THE BOY: Now, my wife and I live downstairs, so no loud parties.

LIZ: Oh, I'm pretty quiet.

THE BOY: We just had a new baby, so my wife -- she's pretty adamant that our tenants respect that.

LIZ: Not a problem. (*Handing HIM the paper.*) You won't even know I'm here, Mr. Baker.

THE BOY: You can call me Nick.

LIZ: Thank you, Nick.

> *HE exits. LIZ looks around, pulls out a notebook.*

LIZ: Here three days and already I found an apartment - downtown Cedar City. Damn! Things are cheap here! It's a big, clean, two bedroom apartment ... and it's about four times less expensive than my place in LA. Best part is, I can take a five minute walk and be completely out of town and into a red rock canyon. The landscape is beautiful here. I'd seen photos, but . . . you just don't know until you've seen it with your own eyes. I once read in an old military handbook that this area was "A damn good place to throw used razor blades."

> *Lights out on LIZ. Lights up on THE GIRL who enters carrying a pie.*

THE GIRL: On behalf of the fourth ward relief society we'd like to welcome you to the neighborhood and offer you this peach pie. Now, Sister Baird made this pie and she's got really got a gift for it. She's won the blue ribbon at State Fair three years running, so you and your husband will just *love* it. (*Beat.*) Oh, you're not married? (*Beat.*) Well, there's a fireside tonight. Why don't you come down with my husband and I, and Bob can introduce you around! There are plenty of nice young men in our singles ward. Now ... how old are you? (*Concerned.*) Oh. (*Beat.*) Well, don't you worry. You've still got time.

> *Lights out on THE GIRL. Lights up on THE BOY. HE walks in quickly.*

THE BOY: (*Kindly*) Okay, now I spoke to the cook and he said he wasn't sure, so I spoke to the manager and she said she thought we had it, but she wasn't sure where. So we called the owner and he said yes, we *do* have one but it's in storage. So he's gonna' have his wife run it down here for you in a few minutes and we'll get it all fired up. But the cook wanted me to ask you if you wouldn't mind showing him how to do it. (*HE leans in, whispers.*) We don't get a lot of orders for coffee.

> *Lights fade on THE BOY. Lights up on THE GIRL. SHE uses a bar towel to wipe down a pint glass.*

THE GIRL

THE GIRL: A shot of what? (*Beat.*) What does that mean, well drink? You mean, like, liquor? 'Cause we ain't got that here. (*Beat.*) Yeah, it's a bar. Don't it look like a bar? (*Beat.*) What's so funny? (*Beat.*) Oh, you from out of state? Well, it's beer only. 3.2 percent. Utah law. No, I'm serious. We got Bud Light, MGD and Corona. And we got some wine coolers. (*Beat.*) Hey look, lady, I don't make the rules. You want the hard stuff you can drive into Arizona. Grocery stores got nothin' but the same stuff we got. It's after 10, though, so they won't be sellin' it again 'til Monday. (*Beat.*) You want a Bartles-n-James or somethin'?

> *Lights out on THE GIRL. SHE exits. Lights up on LIZ, still writing.*

LIZ: This is ridiculous. Utah is driving me insane. I have to drive out of state for a drink, there is NO good Asian food and the damn missionaries won't leave me alone. I've met with May and we're making progress, but I can't rely on just her. I need more stories. It's amazing how ignorant this town is. Half the people I approach don't even know what I'm talking about. How could they possibly not know what happened here?

> *Lights out. LIZ exits. Lights up on MAGGIE and JOE. THEY sit on a blanket, as if outdoors, staring up at the night sky.*

JOE: Have I mentioned lately how glad I am that you're my wife?

MAGGIE: As a matter of fact, yes. You have.

JOE: Then have I mentioned how beautiful you are?

MAGGIE: (*Laughing.*) Yes.

JOE: Then ... have I told you my CO gave me the entire week off?

MAGGE: (*Delighted.*) The whole week?!

JOE: The whole week.

> *MAGGIE grabs JOE and they kiss. They are clearly infatuated and extremely happy. A loving couple.*

MAGGIE: You're not in trouble are you?

JOE: What?

MAGGIE: I mean, he sent you home for the week? Just like that? Did you do something wrong?

JOE: No, no. My whole outfit got the week off. We've been working so hard, and a bunch of the boys have been getting sick.

MAGGIE: Sick?

JOE: Oh, it's nothing. Just a little heat stroke. I mean, we're out there nearly every day in the middle of the desert.

JOE: Have you gotten sick?

JOE: Not bad, no. Some of the boys get it real bad, though. Sweating, coughing, throwing up –

MAGGIE: (*Smacks him playfully.*) Oh, Joe! Don't talk about that. It's disgusting!

JOE: Sorry.

MAGGE: Ew.

JOE: Did you go see that last one? Like I told you?

MAGGIE: Mmm hmm. I went with your folks. We took the blankets out on the west ridge. It was so pretty.

JOE: Didn't I tell you? I love watching them go off. Especially when it's still dark out. They usually let us all go right out there on the test flat to watch. It's so amazing.

MAGGIE: I would love to see it from that close up. We had a pretty good view from out here, though. The whole town went out there to see it.

JOE: Really?

MAGGIE: Practically! Bishop Everett made an announcement. Everybody was talking about it. Even those new sister missionaries came out for it. Some people went higher up, but there were, oh, I'd say about thirty or forty of us on the ridge.

JOE: Wow.

MAGGIE: Everyone's so proud of you, too. I mean, you're practically a scientist!

JOE: I'm hardly that.

MAGGIE: I like the snow.

JOE: The snow?

MAGGIE: Yeah! After that last one we got this ... snow. It was pink. Little pink puffy snowflakes. Your brothers went out and played in it. They had a ball.

JOE: Aw, and I missed it!

MAGGIE: You haven't seen it?

JOE: Naw. The wind's always blowing away from the base when they go off. Oh well. Wish I'd been here with you.

MAGGIE: Me, too. Oh, Joe! I love having you here with me! I love it when you're home.

JOE: It's all I can think about when I'm over there. Just getting home to you.

MAGGIE: You think about me?

JOE: Are you kidding? Every moment! Every second.

MAGGIE: Really?

> *JOE nods emphatically.*

MAGGIE: What do you think about?

> *JOE leans into MAGGIE. THEY kiss.*

JOE: I love you so much.

> *MAGGIE smiles. Beat.*

MAGGIE: I've got something to tell you.

JOE: What?

MAGGIE: (*Teasing.*) Hmmm ... maybe I should wait.

JOE: What? Tell me now.

MAGGIE: I don't know ... I think I'll wait.

> *MAGGIE stands up. JOE jumps up and stops her by playfully grabbing her from behind, his arms around her belly.*

MAGGIE: Joe, careful!

> *JOE immediately lets go of her. MAGGIE turns around, realizing she gave away her secret. We see it dawn on JOE that MAGGIE's pregnant.*

MAGGIE: So ... surprise.

JOE: You're --

MAGGIE nods, smiling.

JOE: Oh, Maggie!

JOE, smiling, is overwhelmed.
Suddenly he picks her up, cradling her
in his arms.

MAGGIE: Woo-hoo! The first of many! Let's go tell everybody!

MAGGIE laughs as JOE carries her
off. Lights fade. THE MAN strolls in.
HE puts on his hat -- again the
military lieutenant. Lights up.

THE MAN: I don't believe I have ever seen anything so beautiful as that shot we set off last week. Just before dawn. I was looking up at that night sky, all the stars, and then ... BAM! Off it went! All the stars just disappeared. Lit up that sky so bright ... (*Pause.*) 'Bout time we started up again. Supposed to have done this one a few days before, but we had to wait for the winds to change. (*Laughs.*) Goddamn! Those folks in Vegas wouldn't have been too happy, would they? Shit ...

THE MAN exits, chuckling to himself.
Lights up on MAY, again in her
rocker. LIZ sits nearby.

MAY: Adverse weather conditions. That's what they called it. I remember it so well because we all went out to see that shot. Packed up some blankets and hiked clear up to the top of that hill over there. Later on they said on the news that the shot had been delayed due to "adverse weather conditions." The winds weren't blowing our way. (*Beat.*) When it finally did go off, we all went back out on the ridge to watch.

LIZ: Did it scare you?

MAY: Well, it was more excitement than fear. The shot was just beautiful. It really was.

> *Lights dim on LIZ and MAY. Lights up center. THE BOY enters as a 50's reporter, carrying a recorder and microphone. JOE enters, crossing the stage.*

THE BOY: You there, private. Did you see the blast?

JOE: (*Crossing to HIM.*) Uh, yes Sir. I did.

THE BOY: Tell our listeners, boy. What's it like, that atomic blast?

JOE: Well, first there's a big bright light. So bright it kinda' blinds you for a second. Then you hear this *boom!* And there's a big rumbling, and the ground starts to shake a little.

THE BOY: And did you get out of the trench to look?

JOE: Yes, Sir we did.

THE BOY: And what did you see?

JOE: Well, it's like the whole desert just comes rolling out toward you, like a big wave. And you've gotta' duck back down quick or you get a mouthful of dirt. Then we saw the blast, and we heard the blast, and it's all bright and rising up toward the sky.

THE BOY: We hear it's quite a sight.

JOE: Yes, sir.

THE BOY: And how did it make you feel?

JOE: (*Thinks.*) It makes me proud to be an American, sir.

> *THE BOY nods approval. Lights out on THE BOY and JOE. THEY exit.*

Lights back up to full on MAY and LIZ.

LIZ: Like fireworks.

MAY: Pardon?

LIZ: First time I saw fireworks, on the fourth of July. They went off and ... all those bright flashes, the noise. I was scared. But my father said it was all okay. Safe. Pretty.

MAY: Safe. That's what we thought.

LIZ: And what happened after the blast?

MAY: We went home. Went on about our day. Later on, as I was out in my garden, this soft pink snow began to fall. Kind of pinkish-gray. Covering my lettuce blossoms like some seasoning and resting on the crowns of my cherry tomatoes.

Soft pink lights on THE GIRL and THEY boy who enter as children. THEY begins to play silently in the background, pantomiming a snowball fight as MAY speaks.

MAY: It fell all over town, blanketing the ground as the children ran outside to play in it. What a site. Just incredible.

LIZ: And that. Did that scare you?

MAY: (*Shakes HER head.*) We didn't know. I mean, you figure they wouldn't publicize something if it wasn't all okay, right?

MAY turns to look at the children, then stands and looks at LIZ.

MAY: I don't feel safe about anything anymore. I don't know what to believe. They made a big deal about it and, well there wasn't much else to do around here. That was the main event. We all went out to watch - brought picnic lunches and waved our little flags ... I mean, why would they call attention to it if it was a bad thing? (*Pause.*) But they were hosing down cars. Just south-west of St. George, they were pulling cars over on the highway and hosing them off for "safety reasons." So you really begin to wonder at this point. What in the world could be safe for children, but harmful to a Buick?

> *THE BOY and THE GIRL dust themselves off and exit, laughing. MAY watches them go. Lights fade. Lights up on THE MAN who enters dressed as a doctor. JOE and MAGGIE enter. MAGGIE wears a hat.*

THE MAN: So, what seems to be the trouble?

MAGGIE: Well, I got this rash. It was ... it was like a sunburn, only worse.

JOE: Just terrible. I've never seen anything like it.

MAGGIE: The thing is, I wasn't really out in the sun.

JOE: She was blistered, you know? Her skin got all red.

MAGGIE: I had this headache that wouldn't go away, and I couldn't keep anything down. Nausea all the time. Anyhow, that went away after a few days, so I didn't think much more about it. Then ...

JOE: I was out in the yard and I heard Maggie calling for me. I ran into the house and she had her brush in her hand. Most of her hair was on the floor.

MAGGIE: It was awful. It all just ... came out. This huge lump of hair.

JOE: Anything else?

MAGGIE: Well ... mostly just the headaches now.

> *THE MAN makes notes on his clipboard. Pause.*

JOE: So, what now? Should she be tested? What?

THE MAN: No, I really don't see a need for that.

MAGGIE: But, what about the baby? I'm two months pregnant.

THE MAN: Oh, no need to worry about that.

JOE: So then, what is it? What do we do?

MAGGIE: I hope I don't sound paranoid, it's just that nothing like this has ever happened before.

THE MAN: (*To MAGGIE.*) You have nothing to worry about. You're going to be just fine. (*Beat.*) I would like to speak to your husband for just a moment, though. Could you excuse us?

> *JOE nods to MAGGIE and SHE exits.*

THE MAN: Joe, your wife has what we refer to as "Housewives Syndrome." (*Beat.*) Neurosis, Joe. Boredom. It's self-inflicted.

JOE: But ... her hair, and the ... I don't see how –

THE MAN: Look, if I were you I would take her home. Get her to rest. Read her some scripture, talk to her. Make sure she's eating right. (*Beat.*) This will pass, Joe. It's really very common.

> *Lights fade. THEY exit. Lights up*
> *again on MAY and LIZ.*

MAY: No, really. Housewives Syndrome. It was diagnosed all the time in the fifties. A bit like "Cabin Fever" maybe? But a hell of a lot more degrading. Anyway, people just started buying into it. I couldn't believe it. It's fitting, though, don't you think? HOUSE wives. You think you're safe. That's how you should feel, right? That's how I felt. The pictures on the walls, the shoes by the door, the quilt on the bed ... what good are they? Maybe we were crazy. Crazy to think those things protected us. Those walls could have been made of cast iron or lace. Wouldn't much matter.

LIZ: And after you realized. Did you still go out to watch?

- 26 -

MAY: No. Not me. Sometimes I would wait in the basement. Didn't help. I mean, I know that now, but ... Well, I suppose I could have stayed down there -- what, for twenty years? Thirty? What kind of life is that? Wouldn't have done any good.

> *THE MAN enters again as a Mormon Bishop and reads from the Book of Mormon, to audience.*

THE MAN: "And ye shall bear it patiently, your reward shall be doubled unto you four-fold."

> *MAY rises, LIZ stands beside her.*

MAY: It was all new to us. We're not unintelligent people. At first we were confused. I mean, in a situation like that ... well, it takes a while to understand it -- to let it in. When I finally did ... Well, I didn't exactly suspect in the right direction. I thought, in the beginning at least, I thought that it was coming from somewhere else entirely.

THE MAN: (*To Audience.*) "And it came to pass there was a great and terrible tempest; and there was terrible thunder, insomuch that it did shake the whole earth as if it was about to divide asunder."

MAY: I thought it was Heavenly Father. I thought it was from God.

THE MAN: "And there were exceedingly sharp lightnings, such as never had been known in all the land."

MAY: We're taught that God works through man. So basically anything that happens is the will of God.

THE MAN: "And there was great and terrible destruction in The Land Southward."

MAY: When that occurred to me, I was so frightened. My faith became stronger than ever. Out of fear.

THE MAN: "And behold, the rocks were rent in twain; they were broken up upon the face of the whole earth, insomuch that they were found in broken fragments, and in seams and in cracks upon the face of the land."

MAY: I remembered something I heard as a child. Something my Uncle read from the scriptures. I thought it was an explanation.

THE MAN: "And it came to pass that there was thick darkness upon the face of the land -- insomuch that the inhabitants thereof who had not fallen could feel the vapor of darkness."

MAY: Book of Mormon, Third Nephi.

THE MAN: "And in one place they were heard to cry and mourn, saying: O that we had repented before this great and terrible day, then would our mothers and our fair daughters, and our children have been spared."

MAY: I thought it was us. I thought we were being punished for something. I mean, nothing happens that God doesn't intend, right?

> *THE MAN freezes. MAY takes the book from THE MAN. HE exits. MAY hands the book to LIZ, points out a passage.*

LIZ: "And many great destructions have I caused to come upon this land, and upon this people, because of their wickedness and their abominations."

> *Blackout. THEY exit. Lights up. MAGGIE sits, staring at the floor. JOE enters.*

JOE: Maggie. (*No response.*) Maggie. (*HE sits next to her.*) Maggie, please. It's time to go. (*Pause. Still no response.*) I'll go get the car.

MAGGE: I won't go.

JOE: Honey, we have to.

MAGGIE: Why? What difference will it make?

JOE: I guess you're right. You can stay if you want. I'd rather you went with me, though.

MAGGIE: No.

JOE: Maggie, you can stay here. That's fine. Everyone will understand. No one will think badly of you, but --

MAGGIE: I don't care what anyone thinks of me.

JOE: Look, it's okay if you don't want to go. But, I think someday you'll wish you had. (*Pause.*) Maggie?

MAGGIE: Why did it happen?

JOE: I don't know, honey. Heavenly Father has a plan though. He has reasons and we're not supposed to understand --

MAGGIE: Why would He take our child, Joe?

JOE: I don't know. We have to trust Him, though. We have to --

MAGGIE: If you can accept that, then you go!

JOE: Damnnit, Maggie! Do you think I don't feel this? I'm struggling, too! It took all the strength I had just to get out of bed this morning. I'm scared to stand. I'm trying to get through, but all of sudden it just hits me and I feel like I'm going to collapse. Do you know how helpless I feel? I'm supposed to protect you. I'm supposed to protect our family. I feel so useless. (*Pause.*) There's nothing we can do about it. I wish we could, but there's nothing. You don't have to go. You don't have to do anything. I can't tell you that's it going to get easier, because I don't know ... maybe it never will. But they're going to bury our daughter today and I'm going to be there with her.

> *Long pause. Finally MAGGIE looks up.*

MAGGIE: I want another baby.

JOE kisses her on the head. MAGGIE looks away. JOE stares at her for a few moments, then exits. Spotlight on THE MAN. HE is dressed again as the Bishop. HE reads from the Book of Mormon.

THE MAN: "Yea, except ye repent, your women shall have great cause to mourn; for ye shall attempt to flee and there shall be no place for refuge; yea, and wo unto them which are with child, for they shall be heavy and cannot flee; therefore, they shall be trodden down and shall be left to perish."

Lights out. THE MAN and MAGGIE exit. Lights up on MAY.

MAY: Suddenly it was everywhere. At first it was just ... I don't know. You couldn't put your finger on it. Something was off, but it took different forms. It was different for everyone. It seemed to reach the children first. Leukemia. Children died. It got to the point where we were holding three or four funerals every week. In a town this small ... well, it's just not right. The doctors hadn't seen it before, so most children were mis-diagnosed. There was mental retardation, too. It used to be that you knew someone who's uncle had a sister-in-law who's son had it -- or something like that. But all at once it was everywhere ... your neighbor's children, your boss' children, your own children. (*Beat.*) It's a terrible thing when a mother out-lives her children. I out-lived all of mine. And my husband. (*Beat.*) Everyone was getting sick.

Lights out.

JOE (V.O.): So, what is it? What do we do?

MAGGIE (V.O.): I hope I don't sound paranoid, it's just that nothing like this has ever happened before.

THE MAN (V.O.): You have nothing to worry about. You're going to be just fine.

Sound of applause. Lights up. Cheesy game show theme music plays. THE

> *GIRL and THE BOY enter and stand on opposite sides of the stage, facing out. As this happens, a stand - as is used for a game show - is rolled in and placed center. There is a bell in the center of the stand.*

ANNOUNCER (V.O.): It's time once again for America's favorite game show, You Bet Your Lives!

> *More applause.*

ANNOUNCER (V.O.): And here is the host of You Bet Your Lives, Dick Newcomb!

> *Still more applause. THE MAN enters carrying a microphone and wearing the cheesy, flashy suit.*

THE MAN: Thank you! Thank you! Ladies and gentlemen, we have a great show for you today! Let's say hello to our guests! (*Turning to THE BOY.*) A professional surfer, representing his hometown of Long Beach, California, let's have a big round of applause for ... Bob!

> *THE BOY waves. More applause. THE MAN turns to THE GIRL.*

THE MAN: And a housewife, representing her hometown of Salt Lake City, Utah, let's say hello to ... Suzie!

> *THE GIRL waves. More applause.*

THE MAN: Now, as you know, we'll be asking our contestants a series of questions worth ten points each. Whoever has the most points at the end of the game - LIVES!

> *Applause.*

THE MAN: Let's start with you, Bob. (*HE pulls out an index card.*) Which town has a higher population? Is it ... (*Beat.*) Tocuerville, Utah? (*Beat.*) Panguitch, Utah? (*Beat.*) Or Los Angeles, California?

THE BOY: Uh ... LA?

Ding! Applause.

THE MAN: That's right! That's ten points for Bob, he's off to a good start!

Applause.

THE MAN: Okay, your turn Sue! Here we go! According to the Atomic Energy Commission, what is a RAD? That's R-A-D RAD. Is it-- (*Beat.*) A unit of absorbed dose of radiation? (*Beat.*) A stream of electromagnetic waves? (*Beat.*) Or nothing anyone in your area should be concerned about?

THE GIRL: Um ... the first one?

Buzzer sound.

THE MAN: Oh! I'm sorry, no. The correct answer was "nothing anyone in your area should be concerned about." No points for Sue. Bob, back to you. Here's your next question. Who would be more likely to live in Southern Utah? Is it ... (*Beat.*) Government officials? (*Beat.*)
Well-known actors and musicians? (*Beat.*) Or sheep herders no one cares about?

THE BOY: Would it be ... sheep herders?

Ding! Applause.

THE MAN: Right again, Bob! Two for two! That brings your score to twenty points!

Applause.

THE MAN: Okay, Sue. Still not on the board, but this next question could change all that. Here we go. According to the Atomic Energy Commission, what should you do in the event of a nuclear emergency? Should you ... (*Beat.*) Evacuate your area immediately? (*Beat.*) Retreat to the nearest sealed fallout shelter? (*Beat.*) Or, duck and cover?

THE GIRL: Um … fallout shelter!

Sound of buzzer.

THE MAN: No! I'm sorry, Sue! The correct answer was DUCK and COVER. We're looking for duck and cover. No points for Sue. (*HE rings a bell.*) Well, that sound signifies the end of round one. It's time for our bonus round. Now, Bob SEEMS to be taking this game under his control but, as you know, our bonus round is worth twenty-five points. It's anybody's game.

> *THE GIRL and THE BOY each approach the stand, place one hand palm down in front of the bell, and the other hand behind THEIR backs.*

THE MAN: And here's today's bonus question. Buzz in if you think you know the answer. Okay, here we go. Who said "*A lie told often enough becomes truth*"?

> *Pause.*

THE GIRL: Lenin

THE MAN: Oh! I'm sorry, Sue. You didn't buzz in. Bob?

> *Pause. THE BOY rings the bell.*

THE BOY: Was it ... Jerry Mathers?

> *Ding! Applause.*

THE MAN: Congratulations, Bob! You're our winner! Say, Skip, what will our winner receive today?

ANNOUNCER (V.O.): Well, Dick, today's winner will receive a year's supply of brylcream, a brand new, super-exciting color television set, and two tickets to the World Series!

> *THE BOY cheers, exits.*

THE MAN: But wait, Sue, I'm sure we have a nice parting gift for you! Tell us, Skip. What do we have for Sue?

ANNOUNCER (V.O.): Well, Sue, just for appearing on our show today, you'll be receiving a lifetime supply of iodine pills!

THE GIRL looks confused, exits.

THE MAN: Well, that's all the time we have for our show. On behalf of Skip Tripoli and myself, I'd like to thank you for joining us today! Tune in again next week when we'll be giving away chemotherapy treatment packages, hula hoops and coonskin caps! Good night everyone!

More applause. Theme music. Lights fade. THE MAN exits. Lights up. MAY is sweeping. THE BOY and THE GIRL run in dressed as children.

THE GIRL & THE BOY: (*Together.*) Mommy! ... We're home! ... Where are you? ... etc, etc.

MAY: Oh! My darlings!

THEY both hug her.

MAY: Where have you been all day?

THE BOY & THE GIRL: (*Together, laughing.*) At school!

MAY: Oh! Is that where you were? I was just starting to worry!

THE BOY: I got a note.

MAY: About what?

THE GIRL: He's in trouble!

THE BOY: Go soak your head, I am not.

THE GIRL: Na na! You're in trouble!

HE takes a swing at HER.

MAY: Stop it both of you. (*SHE begins to read. Then, to GIRL*--) Darling ...

THE GIRL: Yeah?

MAY: Why don't you go to your room?

THE GIRL: Okay. (*Starts to leave, then whispers to BOY*--) You're in trouble!

SHE exits.

THE BOY: Momma, I didn't do anything, I promise.

MAY: Okay. It's alright.

THE BOY: They're just pictures.

MAY: And you drew them in art class?

THE BOY: Yeah.

MAY: Why, honey? Why would you do that?

THE BOY: (*Frustrated.*) She said to!

MAY: Honey, stop. Now, you're not in trouble, okay? I'm not mad at you. I'm just trying to understand.

THE BOY: They're just drawings.

MAY: Okay. Now, sweetheart, all your teacher says in here is that they're inappropriate. Now, what does that mean?

THE BOY: I don't know.

MAY: Sweetheart, what did you draw?

THE BOY: Sheep.

MAY: Sheep?

THE BOY: Yeah. Can I go?

MAY: But honey, why would she get so upset about sheep?

THE BOY: I don't know! I just did the assignment. I don't know why she got mad. Can I please be excused?

MAY: Yes, honey.

> *Lights change as LIZ enters.*

LIZ: How old was he?

MAY: Twelve.

LIZ: And what was he drawing?

MAY: Sheep. Dead sheep. Sheep with holes burned into their flesh. Sheep with their eyes bulging out. Sheep laying dead in a field. Blood, burns --

LIZ: Oh my God.

MAY: It was horrible. He must have seen it walking to school and back. We took him to talk to the Bishop. Peter and I were afraid he would be scarred. We didn't know what to do. He was obsessed with these images.

LIZ: But why would he draw that? He said the teacher told him to?

MAY: (*Pause. With emphasis* --) The teacher told the class to drawn something that makes Utah unique.

> *Lights out. THEY exit. Lights up on THE MAN who is dressed as a farmer. LIZ enters, notebook in hand, and approaches HIM.*

LIZ: Excuse me. Are you Leeland Allsop?

THE MAN: (*Flirty.*)Yes, ma'am.

LIZ: My name is Elizabeth Callaghan. We spoke on the phone.

THE MAN: Pleased to meet you.

LIZ: Do you mind, then, if I ask some questions?

THE MAN: So you're a writer?

LIZ: Yes I am.

THE MAN: And you want to know about the life of a ranch hand, do you?

LIZ: Yes I do. Something like that.

THE MAN: (*Heavily flirting.*)Well, it really ain't woman's work out here. You gotta' be tough. You gotta' be strong.

LIZ: Hmmm. I see.

THE MAN: You write for the papers? I saw one a' them New York Times before. That's one thick-ass paper - I don't know how they find enough news to fill it. Prob'ly make most of it up. That what you write for?

LIZ: No.

THE MAN: Hmph. Didn't think so.

LIZ: So, did you work this ranch in the fifties?

THE MAN: Yes, ma'am.

LIZ: And what can you tell me about the animals dying?

THE MAN: (*Clearly not happy about the question.*) Ma'am?

LIZ: I mean, were you here when it happened? And if so, what were you told about it?

THE MAN: Ma'am ...

LIZ: I'm specifically interested in the period from 1952 through --

THE MAN: (*Angrily.*) Now you listen here, lady. I'm American, full blooded. I ain't no commie, y'hear? I'm good people, that's what I am. Jus' mindin' my own. Now I don't mean to tell no one their business, but you just better stop that kinda' talk.

LIZ: But don't you think it's odd. All those animals just suddenly dying?

> *Pause. THE MAN regains his composure.*

THE MAN: Malnutrition. Bad weather. (*Beat.*) And you can quote me on THAT.

> *HE storms off. Lights out. LIZ exits. Lights up on MAY.*

MAY: The sheep ... well, that was just the beginning. An early warning sign, maybe. Pretty soon the town was crawling with men in suits. They all drove the same big blue cars and blew through our town like they were floating above it, looking down on all of us. Sometimes they would stop over at café for a meal and some hushed conversation, but they never spoke to us. Just went about their business, whatever that was, and moved on. People didn't seem to notice. Or at least they didn't care.

> *Lights out on MAY. SHE exits. Lights up on THE GIRL and THE BOY who sit on the bench. They have a baby carrier with them. LIZ enters, coughing.*

THE BOY: Elizabeth! How are you?

LIZ: Hi Nick, Grace.

THE GIRL: Sounds like you've caught yourself a cold.

LIZ: I'm afraid so.

THE GIRL: Well, don't you worry. Dr. Norton is the best in town.

LIZ: What about you, everything okay?

THE BOY: Oh yeah. Just here to get the baby's extra fingers and toes removed.

LIZ: (*Laughing.*) Oh, right. Of course. (*Beat.*) Really, though. What are you doing here?

THE BOY: We're just here to get her extra fingers and toes removed.

THE GIRL: (*As if this is totally normal.*) Just like her father.

LIZ: Are you serious?

THE BOY: Oh yeah. Take a look. (*HE holds up his hand.*) See the scars? Took one off of here, and here. My father had 'em too.

THE MAN: (*Enters wearing in a lab coat.*) Okay Nick, Gracie. All set?

THE BOY & THE GIRL: (*Together.*) All set!

> THEY exit with THE MAN. LIZ
> remains. Lights shift as MAY enters.

LIZ: I mean, can you believe that?

MAY: It's still here, honey. You bet it is. It's all around you. It's in the gene pool now.

LIZ: But, three generations?

MAY: We pass it on, honey. I passed it on. Breast milk. (*Upset.*) A mother poisoning her own child ...

LIZ: Oh, God.

MAY: (*Almost apologetically.*) We didn't know!

LIZ: So, you were saying ... about the sheep?

MAY: That's right. That's right. Well, it wasn't long after that when I found out about the pills they were handing out in the schools. Some children got them, some didn't.

LIZ: They were ...

MAY: Oh yes. They were testing. My children became their experiment.

> *THE GIRL, THE BOY and THE MAN enter. THEY are all dressed as "hippies", except THE MAN who wears a suit. THEY march in a circle. Each of THEM holds a sign above their head, as if attending a protest rally. The signs read, "NO MORE TESTING," "BAN THE BOMB," and THE MAN's sign reads "COMMIE." Their lips move, as if shouting or chanting, but we hear nothing.*

MAY: I didn't want to pretend anymore that nothing was going on. I couldn't. I didn't set out to change the world. I just wanted to *do* something. I wasn't sure how to begin. I didn't even know if I should. Some people were holding demonstrations. I wanted to go, but people were saying ...

THE MAN: You'd better steer clear of that. Those folks are Communists.

> *THE MAN and the marchers move off stage.*

MAY: Everyone I spoke with told me to bite my tongue. They said everything was fine. I almost believed it. I guess it's easy to believe something if you really *want* to believe it. But eventually you have to see the truth. And that's really all I ever wanted -- the truth. I had to start somewhere, so I got in touch with a doctor out in California. I told him about my Peter's cancer, and he was interested. He asked me to send him Peter's medical records. But I couldn't get them. They wouldn't release them. I just kept thinking ... if there was really nothing to this, why would they try to hide it? They *must* know what's going on.

> *Lights dim on MAY. SHE and LIZ exit.*

JOE (V.O.): So, what is it? What do we do?

MAGGIE (V.O.): I hope I don't sound paranoid, it's just that nothing like this has ever happened before.

THE MAN (V.O.): You have nothing to worry about. You're going to be just fine.

> *THE MAN enters. Once again he wears the Sunday jacket and reading glasses, and carries the Book of Mormon. HE reads to the audience.*

THE MAN: "And ye shall bear it patiently, your reward shall be doubled unto you four-fold."

MAY: (*Walking into the light.*) Why? Why is this happening to so many people? Why hasn't anything happened to me?

> *THE MAN takes no notice of MAY.*

THE MAN: "O all ye are spared because ye are more righteous than they."

> *Lights begin to blackout.*

MAY: Wait!

> *As MAY cries out, lights come back up abruptly. THE MAN looks at MAY, startled.*

THE MAN: (*Jarred by this interruption.*) Yes?

MAY: I don't believe that.

THE MAN: What?

MAY: I don't believe that I'm more righteous than ... (*Pointing to audience members.*) Her ... or him ... or you.

THE MAN: Do you deny the word of God?

MAY: No! It's just that ... well couldn't it be something else?

THE MAN: It is not our place to question the will of God.

MAY: Yes, I know. But, what if this isn't God's will? I mean, this all seemed to start when they opened started that testing facility --

THE MAN: The first law of God is obedience. Let's consult Doctrine and Covenants. (*He opens the book.*) D & C 134. "We believe that governments were instituted of God for the benefit of Man."

MAY: But --

THE MAN: "We believe that all men are bound to sustain and uphold the respective governments in which they reside, and that sedition and rebellion are unbecoming every citizen thus protected, and should be punished accordingly."

MAY: But that's not what I'm saying! I mean, do we just sit back and let them --

> *Suddenly THE MAN hurls the book at the back wall, rips off the jacket and the glasses, and flies toward MAY. Frightened, MAY turns to run off stage, but he catches her, spins her round, and pins her up against the back wall. It is a very violent exchange.*

THE MAN: Now you listen to me! This is not a game. Do you hear me?

> *MAY nods, frightened.*

THE MAN: I've had just about all I can take of this nonsense. From you, from that girl, from everyone! (*Beat.*) Alright?

> *MAY nods again. THE MAN begins to regain his composure. HE loosens his grip. Suddenly HE remembers the*

audience. HE glances toward them,
then lets go of MAY.

THE MAN: (*Completely cool.*)Now run along while I talk with them.

MAY looks worriedly at the audience,
nods, leaves. THE MAN walks toward
the audience.

THE MAN: (*Gathering glasses and jacket.*) I'm sorry about that. I wouldn't have hurt her. I just don't like people to get carried away. I was only looking out for you. No reason to upset you folks, right? That's right. Some people just don't realize that all things have a price. How does it go? Sacrifice one sheep to save the flock? Something like that. Well, how much do you think it costs for a little ... convenience? Or a blind eye? A blind eye toward polygamy perhaps? A blind eye toward a messy little massacre out in the Mountain Meadows? That doesn't come cheap.

HE turns to leave, then turns back.

THE MAN: I hope you're all clear on what's going on here. (*Pause.*) Now you run along. I'll be here when you get back.

Lights fade.

Blackout.

END ACT I

ACT II

> *There is a small table with two chairs*
> *SL and a podium SR, both as yet unlit.*
> *Lights up center. MAGGIE, JOE, THE*
> *GIRL, THE BOY stand with hymnals*
> *again. THE MAN leads them.*

ALL:
(*Singing.*)

> Why should we mourn or think our lot is hard?
> 'Tis not so; all is right.
> Why should we think to earn a great reward
> If we now shun the fight?
> Gird up your loins; fresh courage take.
> Our God will never us forsake;
> And soon we'll have this tale to tell --
> All is well! All is well!

THE MAN: Please turn to first Nephi, Chapter 22, verse seventeen. "Wherefore, he will preserve the righteous by his power, even if it be that the fullness of his wrath must come. Wherefore, the righteous need not fear; for thus sayeth the prophet, that they shall be saved -- even if it be by fire."

ALL: Amen.

> *THE MAN, THE BOY, and THE GIRL*
> *exit.*

JOE: I have to get back.

MAGGIE: You just got here, Joe.

JOE: I'm sorry.

MAGGIE: Joe ...

JOE: What?

> *Pause.*

MAGGIE: Nothing. I love you.

JOE: I love you, too.

> *JOE runs off stage. MAGGIE rocks herself back and forth in silence. BLACKOUT. SHE exits. THE MAN sits at the table, reading a newspaper and drinking coffee. HE wears a suit and a fedora. HE wears an ID badge and we can clearly see the letters AEA (Atomic Energy Commission) displayed on it. Lights up on THE MAN. THE BOY enters dressed similarly, also wearing an AEA badge. HE carries a cup of coffee in one hand and a newspaper under his arm. HE heads toward the table and sits with THE MAN.*

THE BOY: (*Greeting THE MAN.*) Shepardson ...

THE MAN: (*Greeting THE BOY.*) Murphy ...

> *THE BOY is seated now, sips his coffee, and pulls out his paper.*

THE MAN: Take a look at page three.

THE BOY: "French Decline, Secretary Dulles Returns." Wait a minute, the French actually refused us!?

THE MAN: Said they could fight those Goddamn gooks without our bombs. I'd like to see 'em try.

THE BOY: What the hell is wrong with them?

THE MAN: They're French!

> *THEY laugh.*

THE BOY: Eisenhower must be fuming.

THE MAN: You're damn right he is. Offered 'em two of our nukes. Even offered to fly 'em over Viet Nam in our planes. They flat out refused it.

THE BOY: Why?

THE MAN: I don't know ... fallout, the environment, blah, blah, blah.

THE BOY: (*Nodding.*) Oh ... yeah.

THE MAN: (*Surprised.*) Yeah nothing! Who the hell gives a rat's ass? That's half way across the world from us. And the French. Why the hell should we care about a bunch of squinty-eyed bastards?

> *Beat.*

THE BOY: I bet we'll end up in this thing.

THE MAN: Hell yes we'll be in it! Someone's got to jump in and take care of this mess, and it sure as hell won't be any of those goody-goody European faggots.

THE BOY: You think we'll use the nukes?

THE MAN: In a heart beat.

THE BOY: But ... won't that look bad for us? I mean, it might be too soon, right? We're still getting flack for Hiroshima. We don't want to come off looking like trigger-happy monsters.

THE MAN: Son, we're doing it right over this hill. Right here in America's backyard. I mean, yeah, they may be just a handful dim-witted Mormons, but they're American. If we'll do it to our own what makes you think, even for a moment, that we'd give it a second thought half way around the globe in some third-world rice paddy?

> *Pause. THE BOY resumes reading his paper.*

THE MAN: Julie called here yesterday.

THE BOY: Oh? How's she doing?

THE MAN: She's fine. 'Bout to finish up high school.

THE BOY: Already? I always think of her as being five, you know? Wow. Graduating high school, it's hard to believe.

THE MAN: I know it, I know it.

THE MAN: So, is she settling down?

THE MAN: Julie? Hell no. She wants a career. Wants to make her own money. It's a whole new world, my friend.

THE BOY: Good Lord.

THE MAN: She wants to be a teacher.

THE BOY: Well, that's not too bad. Grade school?

THE MAN: Yeah. Get this - she says to me "Dad, I'm going to the Teacher's College over in Cedar City."

THE BOY: Oh, no!

THE MAN: I know. I told her -- don't you dare! I don't want you anywhere near here, darling.

THE BOY: What did she say?

THE MAN: Well, you know Julie. She's got her mother's temper. I guess it's a good school and she thought it would be nice to be closer to me. Anyway, I explained it to her in detail. She understood. We've got her looking at schools back east now.

THE BOY: Thank God.

> *Lights fade. THE MAN crosses to the podium. THE BOY crosses and stands beside him. THE GIRL enters and*

*stands off to the side. She is dressed as
a 1950s newspaper reporter. Lights
up. Flashbulbs.*

THE MAN: No, we are one hundred percent positive on this point. Let me say this again so there is absolutely no misunderstanding. There is positively no correlation -- none at all -- between Nevada's testing and the recent loss of livestock in Southern Utah. The Atomic Energy Commission is on site there simply to study the phenomenon and, hopefully, help in offering some answers to the local ranchers. We are NOT there out of obligation because, as I have stated previously, there is no correlation between our work in Nevada and this bizarre and unfortunate epidemic.

THE BOY: (*Leaning into the podium.*) I'm sorry, ladies and gentlemen, Doctor Shepardson has time for just one last question. (*HE points to THE GIRL.*) Yes, Miss. What's your question?

THE GIRL: Thank you. Doctor Shepardson, there are many people who believe that Nuclear Testing is responsible for the recent steady rise in cancer-related civilian deaths across the state of Utah. What would you say to those people?

THE MAN: (*Slow and steady.*) We are in Nevada conducting these tests under the full support of and with the full cooperation of the United States government and President Eisenhower. We are studying atomic energy for the benefit of all mankind. It is our sincere hope that the tests we conduct today will promote future peace throughout the world. Atomic energy poses absolutely no threat to the health of Americans.

THE MAN: If we were aware of any such threat we would not conduct these tests on American soil --

THE GIRL: What about Doctor Oppenheimer's objections and concerns regarding --

THE MAN: I cannot comment on Doctor Oppenheimer. That is for the House Un-American Activities Committee to decide.

THE GIRL: And what about the --

THE MAN turns and exits.

THE BOY: (*Leaning into the podium.*) I'm sorry, that's all the time we have for today. Thank you.

> *More flashbulbs, general chatter.*
> *Lights fade. ALL exit. Podium is*
> *struck. Lights up on JOE who enters*
> *and collapses. HE breathes heavily.*
> *HE is in full uniform and wears a*
> *small film badge - a device used to*
> *measure amounts of radiation*
> *received - on his breast pocket. THE*
> *MAN enters in military uniform, sees*
> *JOE, and marches over to HIM.*

THE MAN: You okay, Private?

JOE: Uh ... yes sir. I think so.

THE MAN: Good.

> *THE MAN helps JOE to his feet.*

JOE: Thank you, sir.

THE MAN: (*Gazing out at the horizon.*) That was a beautiful shot this morning, wasn't it Private? Biggest one yet, you know.

JOE: (*Coughing.*) Yes, sir.

THE MAN: You okay, boy? What's the matter? Where you supposed to be?

JOE: I was in the trench, sir.

THE MAN: Well, son, they're still out there. You're supposed to be on recon, boy. What are you doing back here?

JOE: They sent me back, sir. I was sick, sir.

THE MAN: Let's see that badge, Anderson.

*JOE removes the badge from his
breast pocket and hands it to THE
MAN. THE MAN glances at it and
hands it quickly back to JOE.*

THE MAN: Shit, son. Ain't nothing wrong with you but a little heatstroke.

JOE: Yes, sir.

THE MAN: You get yourself back to the barracks and cool down. You'll
be alright.

JOE: Yes, sir.

THE MAN: Remember -- the sun's the problem out here, boy. Ain't
nothin' gonna' get you but the sun. Easy to get sick in this goddamned
desert heat.

JOE: Yes, sir.

THE MAN: You get yourself some water. Lots of water, you hear me?

JOE: Yes, sir.

THE MAN: Dismissed.

JOE: Thank you, sir.

*JOE salutes, turns and runs off a bit
awkwardly. THE MAN gazes out at
the horizon. Lights fade. Lights up on
LIZ who sits at desk. SHE is writing.*

LIZ: I just don't get it. I don't understand. How do you turn a blind eye to
something like this? And how did they get away with it?

There is a knocking sound.

LIZ: Come in!

THE BOY enters as Nick.

LIZ: Hey, Nick, how's it going?

THE BOY: We, uh ... my wife was wondering if you might be able to come down and watch the kids for a while. Just an hour or two, if you're not busy.

LIZ: Oh. Sure. I mean, of course. No problem.

THE BOY: We'll pay you.

LIZ: Oh, no. No, that's fine. Is everything alright?

THE BOY: Well, I'm sure it will be. My wife just - well, she's been having a little trouble. Something in her throat. So ... we're just going to go check in with the doctor. You know, get it looked at.

LIZ: Oh God, I'm sorry.

THE BOY: Well, her sister had that Thyroid Cancer, so ... you know, just to be safe.

LIZ: Right.

Pause.

THE BOY: Well, we'll be downstairs. Just come down whenever, and help yourself to anything in the fridge.

LIZ: I'll be right down.

> *THE BOY turns to exit. Lights out on LIZ. SHE exits. MAGGIE enters. Lights up.*

MAGGIE: Two children. I've carried two children. (*SHE motions to the ground in front of HER.*) Here they are. (*Beat.*) My first, Chelsea, was still-born. I knew it right away, because there was no crying. Everyone in the delivery room just got so quiet ... and I knew.

THE GIRL takes a few steps in.
Spotlight.

THE GIRL: I'm sorry, Miss.

SHE exits. Spot out.

MAGGIE: I was about five months along with my second child, Jonathan, when I started to wonder. I couldn't feel anything. Not one kick. Joe tried to tell me it was nothing, but I knew.

THE MAN steps in. Spotlight.

MAGGIE: The doctors called it a ...

THE MAN: Molar pregnancy. In a molar pregnancy, there is actually no child. What develops is, in fact, a mass of ...

Spot out. THE MAN exits.

MAGGIE: .... jelly. What they took out of me, Joe said it looked like a big glob of jelly. Cysts or something. I still don't understand it. No one seemed to know why.

THE GIRL takes a few steps in.
Spotlight on THE GIRL.

THE GIRL: I'm sorry, Miss.

SHE exits. Spot out.

MAGGIE: They told me not to try to conceive any more. But I know Heavenly Father has a child waiting for me. Joe agreed to let me try again. I know I'll get through it this time. I'm going to stay with my sister while Joe's away, and she'll take care of me. I won't budge from that bed. I'm going to have a child if it kills me.

SHE exits. THE MAN marches across
the stage, dressed in his military gear.

THE MAN: We're at war here. That's all there is to it. Every war has its casualties.

> *THE BOY enters and stands beside*
> *THE MAN. JOE enters opposite.*

THE BOY: Okay, listen up. Operation Teapot. We're teaming up with the Food and Drug Administration on this one. We're going to bring in beverages. Common beverages in metal cans. Soft drinks. Beer. We're going to place them out on the test flat during detonation.

THE BOY: Your job will be to collect these items after detonation so they can be re-circulated into the population. We will then be able to monitor and study the effects of radiation on these fluids.

JOE: Yes, sir.

> *JOE salutes, exits.*

THE MAN: We've got opposition.

THE BOY: What do you mean? Who?

THE MAN: Some scientist up in Colorado is causing a fuss.

THE BOY: About Teapot?

THE MAN: About the whole thing. Health and safety concerns. Senator jumped right on that band wagon. Says it's too risky. It's been suggested that we limit our tests to the Pacific.

THE BOY: Perhaps that's wise.

THE MAN: Oh, come on. You knew it was only a matter of time. Besides, do you know how far that would set us back? We can't stop now.

> *THE BOY nods.*

THE MAN: Look, it's not a matter of health or safety with these people. It's a public relations matter. Just a little PR, that's all. Get on with the test.

THEY exit. LIZ enters, sits on bench.
THE GIRL enters, carrying books.

THE GIRL: Are you the lady that called?

LIZ: Yes, Liz Callaghan.

THE GIRL: I'm Aimie Jo. You wanted to ask me some questions?

LIZ: If you don't mind.

THE GIRL: (*Sits on bench.*) Fire away!

LIZ: Okay. You're a student at the University?

THE GIRL: Yeah, I been at SUU for two years now.

LIZ: And were you raised in Cedar City?

THE GIRL: No, I'm from Parowan. It's, like, about twenty minutes up that way.

LIZ: Okay. And how long has your family been there?

THE GIRL: My grandma was born there, but before that I don't know. We're Swedish, though, does that help with your little survey?

LIZ: Uh, sure. So, what I want to ask you is, has anyone in your family ever been effected by the fallout?

THE GIRL: What?

LIZ: Have there been any deformities?

THE GIRL: Ew! No. What are you talking about?

LIZ: Well, radiation has been shown to cause deformities, abnormalities, cancer. Thyroid cancer is probably the most common.

THE GIRL: Oh, I wouldn't worry about that. We've had cancer in my family, but it's just ... you know. The normal stuff.

LIZ: What do you mean by "normal"?

THE GIRL: Oh, come on. Everybody dies of cancer. Plus, there's no, like, radiation stuff around here.

LIZ: I'm actually speaking of fallout from nuclear detonations.

THE GIRL: Oh! Right. That stuff over in Japan. Yeah, that totally sucks. Thank God we live in America, right?

> *Lights out. THEY exit. Lights up on JOE.*

JOE: (*Gravely.*) It s a girl.

> *Lights up on MAGGIE.*
>
> *SHE enters and sits in the rocking chair, holding a bundled baby in her arms. SHE hums.*

JOE: Our daughter was born yesterday. She lived. (*Beat.*) She was born with almost all her internal organs on ... on the outside of her body. (*HE looks at MAGGIE, then away.*) God! I've ... I've never seen anything like it. It was horrible, it was --

> *HE looks up at MAGGIE again - SHE smiles and rocks the bundle, still humming. Lights out on MAGGIE. SHE exits.*

JOE: She's going to have to go through some surgeries. They think, in time, she may even be able to lead a somewhat normal life. My daughter ... (*Beat.*) At first I thought it was me. Then maybe it was Maggie. If it's something else, then I -- No. No! (*HE rips the film badge off his shirt, holds it out.*) You see this? If I had anything to worry about, it'd show up right here.

> *HE looks at the badge, then runs off stage. Lights up. THE BOY, dressed*

> *as a soldier with a film badge, sits at*
> *the table eating. THE GIRL enters*
> *dressed as a waitress. SHE carries a*
> *coffee pot.*

THE GIRL: How you doing? More coffee?

THE BOY: No thanks, I'm all set. Can I get the check?

THE GIRL: Sure. (*SHE sets down the coffee pot and starts writing out the check.*) So, you work out at the proving grounds?

THE BOY: That's right. How'd you know?

THE GIRL: (*Flatly.*) I'm psychic. (*Beat.*) Come on, no one in their right mind would come to Mercury on purpose unless they work out there. I'm just making conversation.

THE BOY: Thanks.

> *SHE rips off the check and hands it to*
> *HIM. HE reaches into HIS breast*
> *pocket, causing HER to notice HIS*
> *film badge.*

THE GIRL: What is that? On your shirt there?

THE BOY: Oh, that's a film badge.

THE GIRL: Yeah, I seen those around. What's it for?

THE BOY: Uh ... it's to measure levels.

THE GIRL: Uh huh.

THE BOY: Radiation levels.

THE GIRL: Hmmm.

THE BOY: (*Handing HER money.*) There you go. Keep the change.

THE GIRL: So, what's your level right now?

THE BOY: Uh ... (*HE looks at the badge, confused.*) Looks like ... well, if I ...

THE GIRL: Mmm hmm.

THE BOY: Well, they have professionals to read these. I just wear it.

THE GIRL: That's real fancy. (*Smirks.*) You have a nice day.

> *THE GIRL exits. Lights out. THE BOY exits. Strike table. Lights up on MAY who sits in the rocker. LIZ is beside her, with a pile of journals and diaries.*

LIZ: Thank you for these journals.

MAY: Twenty years of garage sales. I've been collecting them in my basement. Couldn't bear to see them go to the landfill.

LIZ: (*Flipping through pages.*) How could anyone bear to let go of these? I mean, this is history. Someone's memories.

MAY: Maybe they weren't the kind of memories they were hoping to collect.

LIZ: I'll read them all. Thank you.

MAY: (*Hands a notebook to LIZ.*) And this.

LIZ: Your address book?

MAY: I've marked a few names. They should give you some good information. I doubt you'll be able to quote them officially, but ... maybe you can persuade them. You're very persistent, darling. And thank goodness for it. It's about time people knew what happened out here. (*Points to the notebook, soberly.*) Now, some of those names are crossed off. If you see that, then they've --

LIZ: I understand.

MAY: Look for the ones I've marked. Talk to them.

LIZ: I will, thank you.

MAY: Just don't tell them I sent you.

LIZ: I won't. You have my word.

MAY: Oh, I know. You just have to be careful around here.

LIZ: Did they ... have you had some trouble?

> *Dim lights up on the desk. THE MAN and THE BOY enter and begin tearing through the desk, looking for something. MAY and LIZ cannot see what is happening.*

MAY: You could say that.

> *Papers fly everywhere.*

LIZ: What happened?

MAY: I came home to find them in my house.

LIZ: Who?

MAY: Them. I don't know. Men in suits. They were all over my house, it was horrible. Everything was torn apart. Especially Peter's office.

LIZ: What were they looking for?

MAY: I don't know.

> *Across the stage they tear out desk drawers and leave them.*

MAY: It was my fault. After Peter died I went looking for answers. I started asking questions, speaking out.

LIZ: You joined the lawsuit.

MAY: That's right.

> *THE MAN and THE BOY exit. Lights out on the desk.*

MAY: After my children had ... were gone. I lost everything. Just when I thought I had nothing left to lose.

LIZ: What do you mean?

MAY: My family, my friends, my church --

LIZ: Your church?

MAY: I left the church. After all that had happened ... well, my whole life changed. I guess my beliefs did, too. I don't believe in a God. Not anymore. Actually, I think man destroyed God. That's what I think. Man played God, and God was wiped out.

LIZ: So you blame man for Peter's death.

MAY: Yes. Oh, absolutely. Look at this ...

> *MAY produces the check from her pocket. It is folded and worn ... suggesting she probably always carries it.*

MAY: They gave me a check.

LIZ: Is that it? That's the actual check?

MAY: A goddamned check.

> *LIZ leans in to look at the amount.*

LIZ: Wow. How long have you had that?

MAY: A few years now.

LIZ: And what will you use it for?

MAY: Nothing.

LIZ: Nothing?

MAY: They can't bring him back to me, they can't change what they've done. But at least they could admit it. Apologize. That won't ever happen. But I have this. This proves they killed him. All those years I fought. Everyone close to me died -- my husband, my sisters, my parents, my children. My daughter died just after she finished high school. She doesn't get to go away to college, or fall in love, or have a baby. They took that from her. They *took* it! Twelve of the twenty-eight students in her graduating class were gone by the time they held their first reunion. That's nearly half her schoolmates! They actually held part of the reunion at the cemetery. (*Pause. SHE turns to LIZ, with emphasis* --) We can't let it happen. That is, it happened, but we can't keep looking back. We have to look ahead and say, okay. This was done. But we cannot let it be done ever again. (*Long pause.*) I'm going to see them all again, though ... finally.

LIZ: You mean ... you're --?

> *MAY nods. Lights out on LIZ. THE MAN enters and slowly crosses to stand beside MAY. We hear music begin to play.*

MAY: I'm ready. I've been fighting for so long ... I want to go.

> *SHE now sees that THE MAN is standing beside her, patiently.*

MAY: I'm ready.

> *SHE turns to HIM and HE smiles gently, extending HIS hand. SHE smiles.*

MAY: After all, dyin's just a part of life.

> *SHE takes HIS hand. HE gently guides her off stage. It is very calm, peaceful ... A warm exchange.*
>
> *The music continues. Lights up on MAGGIE who sits again in the rocker. SHE rocks a bundled baby. JOE enters, sullen, and stands beside her. After a moment he reaches out to touch her shoulder. SHE looks up at JOE who reaches out for the child. SHE looks back to the child and carefully hands it to JOE, her head bowed, looking away. JOE holds it for a moment, then pulls the blanket over the child's face, and exits. MAGGIE holds herself and rocks, slowly. Lights out on JOE & MAGGIE.*
>
> *The music continues. LIZ enters, wearing a black jacket, as if coming from a funeral. SHE crosses to the desk, sees the mess stops short and stares. Pause. SHE drops to the ground and begins to pick up HER things. Music fades as THE BOY enters.*

THE BOY: Lizzie? You here?

LIZ: Jerry?

THE BOY: My God, look at this place!

LIZ: Jerry ...

> *SHE crosses to HIM. THEY embrace.*

LIZ: Thank you. Thank you so much for coming.

THE BOY: Are you okay?

LIZ: Yeah. I'll be alright.

THE BOY: What happened?

LIZ: I don't know. It was like this when I got here.

THE BOY: Okay, tell me this doesn't scare you.

> *SHE looks around, shrugs.*

THE BOY: Lizzie, come home. Pack your things and let's go tomorrow.

LIZ: You know I can't.

THE BOY: Why not? Liz, I haven't seen you in almost a year.

LIZ: Don't start.

THE BOY: Well, I'm going to. What are you doing, Liz? I can't do this anymore.

LIZ: That's not fair.

> *LIZ begins to clean up the desk, papers.*

THE BOY: Fair? I can't be in a relationship with someone I never see.

LIZ: But you're here now.

THE BOY: I came to bring you home.

LIZ: Excuse me?

THE BOY: You know what I mean.

LIZ: Jerry, I'm *this* close. I know it.

THE BOY: That's what you said six months ago.

LIZ: But I *am*. The students at the University are looking at my play. They want to put it up. Do you know what that means? To have it go up in *Utah*?

THE BOY: That's great, Lizzie. So, you're done. You got what you wanted.

LIZ: No. I'm not done yet.

THE BOY: You said it yourself, they don't want you here. You don't belong.

LIZ: That doesn't matter. I can't stop now. May is gone. I have to finish this. For her.

THE BOY: What about you?

LIZ: This is for me, too.

THE BOY: Come home. Come back with me.

LIZ: But Jerry, I've got it. I've figured it out.

THE BOY: Liz ...

LIZ: No, listen. It's like those bank robbers who made millions stealing a half-penny at a time. This happened slowly. Sporadically. It was nearly invisible to the world. I mean, if they had marched people off, lined them up, and opened fire -- well then of course something would have been done about it. I mean, you can't ignore that, right? But this ... This was like they shot you, but it took you twenty years to die.

THE BOY: Maybe they're right. Maybe you should just leave them alone. Let them move on.

LIZ: No.

THE BOY: Come on, do you really think it's going to help anything? I mean, there's still people who think the Holocaust never happened.

LIZ: I have to put it all together. All the stories - together. So they can't be ignored.

THE BOY: Why? I mean it, Liz. Why you?

LIZ: Because I'm here. Because someone has to. Because it's mass murder. (*Beat.*) May's gone. She gave this to me. She chose me.

THE BOY: Well, I can't compete with that.

LIZ: Jerry --

THE BOY: You're staying, then?

LIZ: I have to.

> *Pause. HE kisses HER.*

THE BOY: I hope you find what you're looking for.

> *HE leaves. SHE sits.*

> *Lights up on THE MAN who reads again from the Book of Mormon.*

THE MAN: "O how great the goodness of our God, who prepareth a way for our escape from the grasp of this awful monster; yea, that monster, death and hell, which I call the death of the body, and also the death of the spirit."

> *Lights out. THE MAN and LIZ exit. MAGGIE is sits in the rocker, silently rocking. Lights up. JOE enters, carrying a book.*

JOE: My Maggie. My beautiful angel. We lost our little girl. Our third child. She hasn't spoken since. (*Beat.*) I read her diaries. I know that's something you should never do, but I couldn't help it. She hasn't said a word for months. I missed her. (*HE opens the diary.*) Right here she wrote — "I don't even know Joe anymore. Something changed him out there. He won't talk to me, barely looks at me. I don't think things will ever be the way they were."

Lights on MAGGIE fade. SHE exits.

JOE: How could I tell her what I saw out there. How do I find the words for that, I mean ... I'm not even sure what I saw. (*Beat.*) They built this little town, see? So they could find out what would happen to houses, banks, school busses. They even put little mannequins out there - little plastic people just standing around this make-believe town in the middle of the desert. After one of those tests my unit was assigned to sweep the area. We were out there for a while cleaning up when we -- (*Beat.*) Cages. I saw cages. I saw them with my own eyes! Animals. Rabbits, goats, pigs ... in cages right out there on the test flat. Burned so bad you couldn't tell -- (*Pause.*) They were looking at them, taking pictures and then just tossing them into the back of these trucks. Just throwing them in there. But they weren't dead yet. And the pigs were squealing so loud -- (*Beat.*) We all looked at each other, but no one said anything. Tex started to cry, but someone shoved him and he stopped. We all just stood there. And Tex was whimpering. (*HE starts to lose his composure, then, with conviction --.*) Something else was out there, behind a fence. They weren't mannequins. I couldn't tell for sure, but they looked like -- (*Getting upset.*) Oh God. God help me if they were. (*Pause. HE regains composure.*) I got sick after that. Officially I had "heat stroke." It was bad this time. Really bad. They took me to the camp medic. Then to the Chaplain.

THE BOY enters in military gear. HE wears a cross. HE helps JOE to the bench. JOE sits.

THE BOY: Joe, come now. You've been very ill. Sometimes the mind plays tricks on us.

JOE: No, I ...

THE BOY: It must have been horrible. I have no doubt that you really believe this hallucination, but --

JOE: Where's Tex?

THE BOY: Who?

JOE: He'll tell you, if you ask him. If you just find Tex --

THE BOY: Joe, no one else saw anything.

JOE: But I --

THE BOY: Joe, it's not uncommon. You've been through quite an ordeal. The heat stroke, Joe. In a fevered state, our dreams become erratic, and they sometimes seem very real.

JOE: No --

THE BOY: We'll get you rested, get you some fluids, and soon you'll forget all about it.

THE BOY exits.

JOE: I must have been out for days. When I woke up I was back in the barracks. On the day I went home, they told me --

THE MAN enters.

THE MAN: You are not to repeat that story of yours. Do you understand what I'm saying to you? Do you understand me, Joe?

JOE: Yes.

THE MAN: Good. (*Beat.*) You have a wife, don't you Joe?

JOE: Yes, sir.

THE MAN: Children?

JOE: (*With difficulty.*) Not yet, sir. But, we're trying.

THE MAN: Oh, that's nice. That is nice, Joe. I would imagine your family is ... important to you. Yes?

JOE: Yes, sir.

THE MAN: Good. You take care, Joe.

JOE: Thank you sir.

THE MAN exits. JOE stands.

JOE: (*To the Audience.*) I never told anyone what I saw.

Lights out. HE exits. Lights up. The table is reset. LIZ enters and sits at the table. THE GIRL enters dressed as the waitress again, but we should see somehow that she is older. SHE carries a coffee pot.

THE GIRL: You want coffee?

LIZ: (*Extremely eager.*) Oh God! Yes, please. Coffee.

THE GIRL: Whoa. Okay ...

LIZ: Sorry. Sorry, it's just that I've been in Utah.

THE GIRL: I'm sorry to hear that. You want something to eat?

LIZ: Can I ask you a question?

THE GIRL: You just did.

LIZ: Right. Could I ask you ... several questions?

THE GIRL: Shoot.

LIZ: How long have you worked here?

THE GIRL: I been here as long as the damn diner, honey.

LIZ: You know about the test site?

THE GIRL: What about it?

LIZ: How do you get in?

THE GIRL: (*Starts to leave.*) Oh, get out a' here.

LIZ: Wait! I just need to know how to get in there. What's the best way?

THE GIRL: What do you think, there's some super-secret trap door or somethin'?

LIZ: Just tell me. Please. How do I get in?

THE GIRL: Easy, girlfriend. You just walk your skinny ass right through that gate down there. Go ahead.

LIZ: (*Handing HER some money.*) Obviously, I'd like to be a bit more discreet than that.

THE GIRL: Are you out a' your damn mind, lady? You might as well walk right in.

LIZ: But I --

THE GIRL: Ain't no being discreet around here. Got that? Go on. Have your fun, honey. There's men in watch towers everywhere. They got lasers or something', I dunno'. But you stick so much as a big toe across that fence, you'll be locked up so tight it'll take an earthquake to get you out.

LIZ: Come on. Come on! I know there's got to be some way --

THE GIR: There ain't. (*Hands the money back to LIZ.*) Trust me honey, please. For your own good. There AIN'T.

> *THE GIRL exits. Lights out. Strike table. LIZ rises and walks forward, holding a sign -- but we can't yet see what it says. Lights up.*

LIZ: When I first visited the Nevada Testing Facility I was 23. Why would I care? Why would you care? There's this map. A map that shows all the places in the country that got fallout dumped on it. Anywhere with enough fallout to cause death is shown in black. (*SHE holds up the map. Almost all of it is covered in black.*) Ever seen this before? (*Beat.*) We're all in this. It hit everyone. Effected everything. We're all downwinders. This is OUR story.

> *THE GIRL and THE BOY enter with protest signs. THEY stand upstage and move in -- protesting silently.*

LIZ: I told my mother I was going to get arrested for spring break that year. That I was going to trespass onto the test site and take some pictures. She didn't like the idea, of course, but she knew better than to try and stop me. So I did it. (*Beat.*) I wasn't ready for it. It wasn't that I was standing on a grave, but at the source of death. It was like ... God, I don't know what it was like. The silence was overpowering. When you stand in a place of evil like that, you have to be ready for it. You have to be capable of facing it. You have to be free of your own evil, or it finds that breach in your armor and the poison seeps in.

LIZ: It changed me. That's why I'm here. That's why I'm still here. Ralph Waldo Emerson once said, "People only see what they are prepared to see." Don't know me. Don't remember me. Don't even look at me. I'm no one. It doesn't matter. Know this ... (*SHE holds up HER sign, moving back toward the protest.*) Know this.

> *LIZ stares straight ahead, over the audience. THE MAN enters. HE is dressed in police attire. HE walks to LIZ, turns HER around, and spreads HER arms and legs. THE BOY and THE GIRL back off stage. HE pulls HER arms behind HER back and handcuffs HER. LIZ stops and turns to HIM.*

THE MAN: You think I'm a monster, don't you?

LIZ: I won't be quiet. I'm going to tell this story.

THE MAN: (*Beat. Serious, hopeful.*) I'm counting on it.

LIZ is taken back by this comment.
THEY share a very important look.
HE then guides HER ahead of HIM.
THEY exit. Lights up on MAGGIE
who is in the rocker, USL platform.

MAGGE: Joe. Joe!

JOE: (*Running to HER with a blanket.*) I'm right here. I've got it, I've got
it.

MAGGIE: Thank you. Mmm ... that's better. So cozy!

JOE: You sound better. Are you feeling better?

MAGGIE: (*Upbeat.*) You know, I am. I really am. I think it might be
turning around.

JOE: That's great, honey. I'll bet you're right.

THE MAN enters. Only JOE sees
HIM.

THE MAN: (*With sincerity.*) I'm sorry, Joe.

MAGGIE: Who knows? Maybe I'll be able to come home soon.

THE MAN: I give her a day or two ... a week at the most.

MAGGIE: I want to sleep in our bed. With you next to me.

THE MAN: Her body's had all that it can take, Joe. I'm sorry.

THE MAN exits.

JOE: I'm glad you're feeling better, honey.

JOE backs away from MAGGIE.

JOE: (*To audience.*) I don't know what to do. I don't know if I should say
anything. Maggie was a good woman. She was all that was good and pure

and beautiful in this world. We ended up having a child. Michael ... he lived. We kept waiting for the doctors to find something, but ... my God! He's healthy! (*HE looks back at MAGGIE.*) That night, just as the sun was setting, she turned to me and said –

MAGGIE: I'm tired baby. I'm going to rest now.

Lights out on MAGGIE. Beat.

JOE: I realize life doesn't always turn out the way you plan, but is it really too much to ask? All we wanted was a little perfection -- just enough! A house, children, happiness. I would give anything if we could start over. I would have taken her away from here. Some place where she would have been safe.

I didn't know. Not at first. You have to believe that. Actually, I was thrilled. It was exciting! Just imagine it ... it was 1949. It was new, it was big. All I knew was what I had seen up to that point -- and that wasn't much. I was the son of a farmer, living just south of the middle of nowhere. I was a hard worker, though, and that's what the service saw in me. I didn't ask questions. I did what I was told, and I did it well. What I saw ... well, it wasn't right. I knew that. But, somehow I let myself be convinced that it was all okay. I was a believer. I believed in my Government. I was used. We all were. I should have questioned it. I should have thought for myself. I don't blame anyone else for my lot in life. The world lays out traps for us and we walk right into them. It's effortless. It would have been so easy to speak up. At least it seems that way now. Back then ... what could I do? One man. I kept my mouth shut. But the more quiet you get, the more you hear. And still I said nothing

The test site is quiet now. Maybe a few random tourists. The bombs are gone, but ... lung cancer, skin cancer, thyroid cancer, leukemia ...

Eventually they admitted we were directly targeted. They told us they had known all along what would happen. And the downwinders? We were expendable.

JOE: When Maggie died, I put my son in the car and we drove west. I drove until I saw the ocean, and I never went back.

*Pause. Lights dim. JOE exits. Lights
up on LIZ. She is older. She sits alone
at an empty table. Stacks of books in
front of HER. SHE looks around. Taps
a pen. Looks around again. Eventually
SHE drops her head on the table. THE
GIRL enters.*

THE GIRL: Miss Callaghan? (*Tapping LIZ.*) Miss Callaghan?

LIZ: Yes?

THE GIRL: It's six o'clock. The store is closing. I've got to clean up.

*SHE stands and begins to gather the
books.*

THE GIRL: Oh, you can just leave those. I'll re-shelve 'em.

LIZ: Oh, okay. Thanks.

THE GIRL: I've gotta' dust 'em anyway.

*LIZ stops and stares at her books.
THE GIRL realizes her comment was
rude.*

THE GIRL: Oh. I mean ... I just meant, that's store policy, you know?
Every book signing. Gotta' dust 'em! 'Cause they can get ... dirty. You
know.

LIZ: Don't worry about it.

*THE GIRL picks up the books. LIZ
begins to leave.*

THE GIRL: Hey, would you sign a copy for me?

LIZ: (*Smiles.*) Sure.

> *THE GIRL hands LIZ a book, LIZ begins signing.*

LIZ: Thank you so much. This makes the whole day worth-while, really.

THE GILR: Cool

LIZ: You know, I gave up four years of my life writing this. It's nice to know somebody wants to read it. (*Hands HER the book*) There you go.

THE GIRL: Thanks! Yeah, I read your flyer and I thought maybe my boyfriend would like it. He's totally into sci-fi.

> *Pause.*

LIZ: You're kidding me.

THE GIRL: No, he totally loves this stuff.

LIZ: (*Sarcastically.*) Great. Well, enjoy.

THE GIRL: Thanks!

> *THE GIRL exits. LIZ turns and starts to walk off. JOE enters as MIKE. MIKE is in his 20's, dressed appropriately for 2003 Los Angeles. HE runs in and stops her.*

MIKE: Excuse me. Are you Elizabeth Callaghan?

LIZ: Who's asking?

MIKE: Oh, sorry. (*Offers HIS hand.*) I'm Mike Anderson. I came for the signing.

LIZ: (*Shaking MIKE's hand.*) Pleased to meet you, Mike.

MIKE: I'm a little late, but they said you were still here, so --

LIZ: Don't worry about it.

MIKE: I brought my own copy. Can I still get it signed?

LIZ: Of course. (*SHE takes the book from him, begins to sign.*) So, are you from LA?

MIKE: Uh, yes. Not originally. My father and I moved here when I was five.

LIZ: From ... ?

MIKE: Utah.

LIZ: (*Looks up.*) Oh.

MIKE: Yeah. My parents grew up there. St. George.

LIZ: And are they ... ?

> *MIKE shakes his head "no."*

LIZ: I'm sorry.

MIKE: Can you sign it to my daughter? Margaret.

LIZ: Sure.

> *SHE finishes, hands the book to HIM.*

MIKE: (*Reads the inscription. It moves HIM.*) Thank you.

LIZ: Are you okay?

MIKE: Yeah. I just -- (*Pause. With feeling--*) Thank you. For writing this.

LIZ: (*Sincerely touched.*) Wow. Thank *you*.

MIKE: (*Close to tears.*) Sorry. I just get so ...

LIZ: I know.

MIKE: (*Regaining HIS composure.*) Thank God it's over.

Pause.

LIZ: Thank God.

> *Lights out on THE BOY and LIZ.*
> *THEY exit. Lights up on THE MAN.*
> *HE sits at a desk wearing a modern-*
> *day suit. HE is a news anchor. We*
> *hear "evening news" music.*

ANNOUNCER (V.O.): This is channel five, eyewitness news for May 23rd, 2003. And now, here's Richard Newcomb ...

THE MAN: Thank you, Skip. Here is tonight's top story ... (*Turns as if to face a camera.*) The United States House and Senate voted this afternoon to lift the Nuclear Test Ban Treaty. President George W. Bush put his stamp of approval on a bill allocating millions of dollars to re-open the Nevada nuclear test site facility, 65 miles northwest of Las Vegas. The measure includes 7.5 million dollars to study the possibility of developing so-called "bunker-busting" nuclear bombs. White House sources say that testing could resume in as little as one year. (*Pause. To Audience, pointedly --*) And now, back to you ...

Blackout.

CURTAIN.

DARCY HOGAN: Born in Upstate New York, raised in Utah, Darcy's 25-year acting and directing career has included four seasons with the Tony Award-winning Utah Shakespearean Festival, and various theaters throughout New York, California and Utah.

www.ingramcontent.com/pod-product-compliance
Lightning Source LLC
Chambersburg PA
CBHW072232170526
45158CB00002BA/869